21st Century
Basic Skills
Library

THE WORLD AROUND US
RIVERS

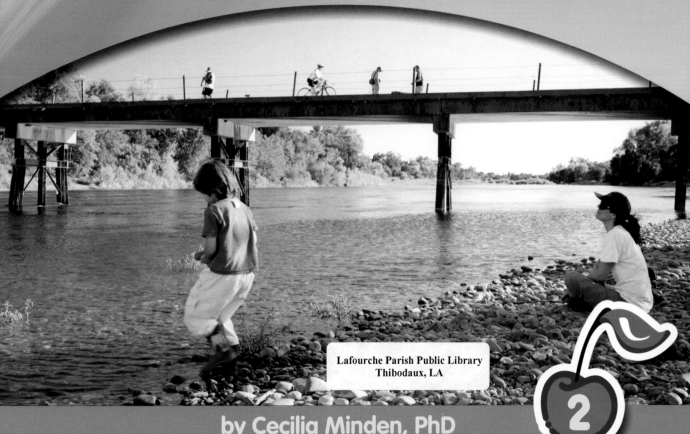

by Cecilia Minden, PhD

Cherry Lake Publishing • Ann Arbor, Michigan

2

Published in the United States of America
by Cherry Lake Publishing
Ann Arbor, Michigan
www.cherrylakepublishing.com

Photo Credits: Cover and page 1, ©iStockphoto.com/slobo; page 4,
©Vaclav Volrab/Shutterstock, Inc.; page 6, ©Heidi Jansen/Shutterstock,
Inc.; page 8, ©Tudor Stanica/Shutterstock, Inc.; page 10, ©Cucumber
Images/Shutterstock, Inc.; page 12, ©Pinosub/Shutterstock, Inc.; page 14,
©E.G.Pors/Shutterstock, Inc.; page 16, ©B.G. Smith/Shutterstock, Inc.;
page 18, ©Simon Krzic/Shutterstock, Inc.; page 20, ©iStockphoto.com/
travelphotographer

Library of Congress Cataloging-in-Publication Data
Minden, Cecilia.
   The world around us: rivers/by Cecilia Minden.
     p. cm.—(21st century basic skills library: level 2)
   Includes bibliographical references and index.
   ISBN-13: 978-1-60279-861-8 (lib. bdg.)
   ISBN-10: 1-60279-861-3 (lib. bdg.)
   1. Rivers—Juvenile literature. I. Title. II. Title: Rivers. III. Series.
   GB1203.8.M56 2010
   551.48'3—dc22   2009048590

Cherry Lake Publishing would like to acknowledge
the work of The Partnership for 21st Century Skills.
Please visit www.21stcenturyskills.org for more information.

Printed in the United States of America
Corporate Graphics Inc.
July 2010
CLFA07

TABLE OF CONTENTS

5   **What Do We Know About Rivers?**

11   **Who Lives in Rivers?**

15   **What Can You Do on a River?**

22   Find Out More

22   Glossary

23   Home and School Connection

24   Index

24   About the Author

What Do We Know About Rivers?

Rivers have a **headwater**.

This is where the river starts.

Rivers flow **downhill**.

Rain and snow add more water.

This makes rivers grow bigger.

The end of a river is the **mouth**.

The river goes into other water.

Who Lives in Rivers?

Animals like to use rivers.

They come for food.

They use them as bathtubs!

You can find many fish in rivers.

Some are good for you to eat.

Others are food for other animals.

What Can You Do on a River?

Ships and boats use rivers.

They carry **cargo** to towns and cities.

15

Some people like to camp or picnic by rivers.

Others like to swim or fish.

You can go **tubing** on a slow river.

You can go **rafting** on a fast one.

What will you do on the river?

Find Out More

BOOK

Sidjanski, Brigitte, and Bernadette Watts (illustrator). *The River*.
New York: Penguin Young Readers Group, 2008.

WEB SITE

Wild and Scenic Rivers Fun Facts
www.rivers.gov/kids/funfacts.html
Read fun facts about rivers and play some river games.

Glossary

cargo (KAR-go) boxes, crates, and other things on a ship

downhill (down-HIL) moving from a higher place to a lower place

headwater (hed-WAW-ter) place where a river begins

rafting (RAFT-ing) traveling down a river in a small boat

rivers (RIV-urz) large, flowing bodies of water that usually empty into seas or oceans

tubing (TOO-bing) floating down a river while sitting in a rubber tire tube

Home and School Connection

Use this list of words from the book to help your child become a better reader. Word games and writing activities can help beginning readers reinforce literacy skills.

a	eat	lives	snow
about	end	makes	some
add	fast	many	starts
animals	find	more	swim
and	fish	mouth	the
are	flow	of	them
as	food	on	they
bathtubs	for	one	this
bigger	go	or	to
boats	goes	other	towns
by	good	others	tubing
camp	grow	people	use
can	have	picnic	water
cargo	headwater	rafting	we
carry	in	rain	what
cities	into	river	where
come	is	rivers	who
do	know	ships	will
downhill	like	slow	you

Index

animals, 11, 13

bathing, 11
boats, 15

camping, 17
cargo, 15
cities, 15

downhill, 7

fish, 13

fishing, 17
flow, 7
food, 11, 13

growth, 7

headwater, 5

mouth, 9

people, 17, 19
picnics, 17

rafting, 19
rain, 7

ships, 15
snow, 7
swimming, 17

towns, 15
tubing, 19

water, 7, 9

About the Author

Cecilia Minden is the former Director of the Language and Literacy Program at the Harvard Graduate School of Education. She currently works as a literacy consultant for school and library publishers and is the author of more than 100 books for children.